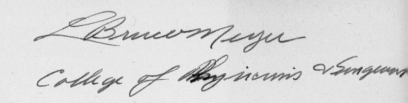

COLUMBIA

An
American University
In Peace And War

COLUMBIA

An
American University
In Peace And War

Fon W. Boardman, Jr.

COLUMBIA UNIVERSITY PRESS
NEW YORK : MORNINGSIDE HEIGHTS
1944

FOREWORD

THIS brief but admirable survey of the history of Columbia University in the City of New York, with special reference to its part in the wars of our country, is one more contribution which the University is happy to make toward complete coöperation with the Government of the United States in the world-wide war of defense which is now raging. The book has been prepared primarily for those young Americans who as students at Columbia in the courses of instruction established here by the United States Navy have been preparing to take personal part in this titanic struggle.

On its pages they will find the story of how the once small and almost rural King's College in the Province of New York has grown to become, in less than two hundred years, the outstanding center of intellectual life, scientific research, and public service which the University now is. This extraordinary development from small and simple beginnings is one more evidence of what has proved to be possible in America in many different fields of endeavor. Beginnings may have been small in many undertakings, whether commercial, industrial, financial, educational or other, but despite that fact the achievements have been literally stupendous. It is important that those young men of today who are going into government service should know, with some accuracy and definiteness, the story of some, at least, of these developments.

This volume which has been prepared under the guidance of our Alumni Federation has been made possible by the generous aid of Henry Krumb of the Class of 1898 and of David W. Smyth of the Class of 1902, to whom the thanks not only of the University itself but of every reader of this book are due.

NICHOLAS MURRAY BUTLER

Columbia University
April 1, 1944

CONTENTS

I. PARK PLACE TO PEARL HARBOR

The First Hundred Years

THE year was 1754. The French had erected Fort Duquesne, out in western Pennsylvania where Pittsburgh now stands, and the governor of Virginia had sent one of his young citizen-soldiers, Lieutenant Colonel George Washington, to meet the French threat. Washington's expedition ran into difficulties; he constructed Fort Necessity at Great Meadows and was forced to surrender it to the French. Thus did war break out. Now known as the French and Indian War, it preceded its European counterpart, the Seven Years' War, by two years, and turned out to be the show-down clash between France and England for North America.

In that same year the Albany Congress met on the banks of the Hudson with commissioners from seven of the American colonies present to treat with the Iroquois in view of the impending conflict. The Congress went further than merely concluding a treaty with the Indians, and discussed a joint arrangement for security against war and invasion. The first step toward union of the colonies had been taken.

Down at the mouth of the Hudson, New York City, although not in 1754 the largest city in the colonies, was a cosmopolitan center of many races, languages, and religions. But while the Dutch had settled New Amsterdam in the early days of colonization, more than a century passed before the Dutch-English colony was able to boast of an institution

THE FACULTY AND STUDENT BODY OF KING'S COLLEGE

President Johnson Teaching the First Class

of higher learning. Commerce had been the chief interest of the colony from the start when a Dutch trading company founded it, and the English who took over in 1664 continued to be absorbed in mercantile affairs. In the 1740s in fact, when there first was serious talk of starting a college in New York, it was said that the whole province could count only fifteen college-trained men in addition to the clergy.

Back in 1703 Trinity Church had offered to deed part of

its church farm for a college campus, but nothing further of importance happened until 1746, when the Colonial Legislature authorized the first of a series of lotteries "for the advancement of learning and towards the founding of a college"; in 1751 some £3,443, raised in this manner, was turned over to a group of trustees to be held for the college. Three more years passed until, on October 31, 1754, King George II granted a charter to "The College of the Province of New-York in the City of New-York in America." Better known as King's College, this was eventually to become Columbia University in the City of New York.

The enterprising first president, and first teacher, of King's College had, however, stolen a march on his Britannic Majesty. Three months or so before the College actually had its charter in hand, Dr. Samuel Johnson, acting for the lottery trustees, had gathered together eight students in the vestry room of the new schoolhouse adjoining Trinity Church on lower Broadway, and there he began instruction. Tuition was twenty-five shillings each term. Johnson, a Yale graduate and at the time of his selection an Anglican clergyman of Stratford, Conn., set about designing a seal for the College and in 1755 doubled the faculty by taking on his son William as a tutor. The next year Leonard Cutting, a Cambridge graduate, was added, and in 1757 the faculty reached four when Daniel Treadwell, a Harvard man, was appointed to the first professorship, that of mathematics and natural philosophy.

King's College still did not have a home of its own. In 1756, on land given by Trinity Church, Sir Charles Hardy, governor of the province, had laid the cornerstone for a building that would be the College's own, but it was not ready for classes until 1760. There, until the Revolution, students roomed, boarded, and studied, with a pleasant view of the Hudson some 150 yards away from the wooded, elevated site of the building.

The young College grew slowly while the storms of the

[3]

"GEORGE THE SECOND, BY THE GRACE OF GOD . . ."

The Royal Charter of King's College

Revolution gathered. As early as 1763 a student had played a major role in one of the first shaking of fists across the sea. Parliament had passed the Stamp Act and the reaction to it in New York resulted in a Stamp Act Congress which sat in City Hall and drew up a declaration of rights. This declaration was based on a draft written by a young New Yorker named John Jay, who would receive his degree from King's College the following year, and who would one day become the first Chief Justice of the Supreme Court.

The College also acquired a new president, its second, in 1763. He was the Reverend Myles Cooper, aged only twenty-six, but already a brilliant scholar hailing from Oxford. During his administration the Medical School, the second in North America and the first to grant an M.D., was established. Cooper's reign was successful enough until he, too, became involved in the approaching Revolution. Cooper was a militant Tory and he came to grips with an equally militant patriot, an undergraduate named Alexander Hamilton. Hamilton not only won the argument, he saved Cooper from possible bodily harm when, on a May night in 1775, he detained a hostile mob of Sons of Liberty on the front steps of the College while President Cooper, attired only in his nightshirt, slipped silently out the back door. The next day Cooper was rowed out to a British warship in the harbor, sailed shortly for England, and was seen no more by King's College.

The Revolution put an end to the first phase of the College's life. In April, 1776, by order of the Committee of Safety, the College was forced to give up its building for hospital purposes. For a short time teaching was continued in a private residence on Wall Street, but after that King's was, until independence was won, dead for all practical purposes. Both American and British troops in turn used the College building, sometimes as a hospital, sometimes as a barrack. It fortunately escaped the great fire of 1776 but it

[5]

was a ruin when restored to the trustees in 1784. Books, apparatus, and equipment had been placed in City Hall for safety, but little was recovered. It seems the British soldiers discovered that most of the articles could be traded for grog in the town's taverns.

With the end of the war, the College came to life with little delay. In 1784 the powers which had previously belonged to the trustees acting under the royal charter were vested in the newly created Regents of the University of the State of New York. Under their auspices the College was reopened, but the fervor of newly won independence would not allow the hated royal tone of the College's pre-war name to remain. King's became Columbia.

But government by the Regents did not prove practical and ended in 1787 when a revised charter of the State Legislature created "The Trustees of Columbia College in the City of New-York," and made the governing body independent and self-perpetuating, which it has remained to this day. These trustees proceeded to select for the presidency one of the first nonclerical college presidents in the English-speaking world, lawyer William Samuel Johnson of Connecticut, son of the first president, who had just finished his work as a member of the Constitutional Convention and was about to become the first United States senator from Connecticut.

When Columbia reopened after the war, the first student entered as a junior. He was DeWitt Clinton, later governor of New York, and guiding spirit of the building of the Erie Canal. The Commencement exercises of that first class were held in 1786 in St. Paul's Chapel, which still stands at Broadway and Fulton Street, and were attended by the members of the Continental Congress. Three years later an even more distinguished audience was present—President George Washington and the members of his cabinet. This was to be the last time until 1902 that a president of the United States paid an official visit to Columbia. In that year Theodore

Roosevelt came to Morningside Heights for the inauguration of his friend and former fellow student, Nicholas Murray Butler, as Columbia's twelfth president.

Columbia in the years immediately after the Revolution was, for a variety of reasons, a small college. In 1787 there were thirty-nine students, only five of whom lived in the College building. In the period from the end of the war to the middle of the nineteenth century Columbia for the most part marked time.

Forty Years at Forty-Ninth Street

In 1849 Columbia had another new president. He was the energetic Charles King, who had been a merchant and editor of the *New York Courier and Enquirer,* and who thus became the first businessman to head the institution. Under King a Law School was established in 1858 and the College of Physicians and Surgeons was united with Columbia in the following year.

But the outstanding event of King's tenure was the re-

KING'S FIRST HOME OF ITS OWN
The Original College Building at Park Place

THE HORSE CARS WENT RIGHT BY THE DOOR
Hamilton Hall at 49th Street

moval of Columbia from downtown Park Place to a site that was far uptown and practically rural in those days—49th Street and Madison Avenue. This was in 1857. In the spring the senior class marched up Broadway to occupy for three months the buildings of the new campus. The move to this particular site was not made, however, without considerable discussion and consideration of other possibilities. For a time it appeared that Columbia would move to the site of the Elgin Botanic Garden, which had been granted to Columbia by the State Legislature in 1814, but the trustees decided against it. Columbia still owns this property, and calls it the Upper Estate, but it is better known as the site of Rockefeller Center, and brings in nearly $4,000,000 yearly in rent.

At 49th Street Columbia did not have to build a new home. The trustees bought the property from the New York Deaf

[8]

and Dumb Institution and the existing buildings were put in shape for what was supposed to be temporary use. This turned out to be forty years. The largest of these buildings was a four-story stucco-covered brick structure. The stucco, though, was already partly peeled off and Columbia students soon referred to it irreverently as the *Maison de Punk*. A new college building, the original Hamilton Hall, was erected in 1879. There was a chapel and a library, the number of volumes being rather limited, partly because the librarian seems to have been most interested in seeing how much of his appropriation for books he could avoid spending. Then, too, there was a janitor (and assistant librarian) who, judging by pictures which have come down to us, was considerably better dressed than most of the faculty members. The College possessed no gymnasium in those days, but the students used John Wood's Gymnasium on East 28th Street. It was in this gym that George Lockhart Rives trained the first Columbia crew, that of 1873. Graduates who attended Columbia during its forty years at 49th Street still perpetuate the memory of those days in their own exclusive association, The Society of the Last of the Forty-Niners.

Columbia was a steadily growing institution until the Civil War disrupted civilian life. Then, in 1864, as the war approached its end, the College received into its presidential chair a distinguished scholar and administrator who was also, fortunately for Columbia, a prophet and a dreamer. He was gaunt, bewhiskered Frederick Augustus Porter Barnard, Yale graduate, one-time professor at the University of Alabama and president of the University of Mississippi, whose deafness did not prevent him from leading the small college a long way on the path to becoming a great university. To stimulate scholarly effort many prizes, scholarships, and fellowships were founded. Under Barnard the School of Mines, first in the country, and the School of Political Science were established.

[9]

The most acrimonious, if not the most momentous, debate over Barnard's policies and plans arose when the precedent-breaking president proposed the admission of women to Columbia. The trustees fought Barnard's efforts, and it was not until 1883 that he wrung from a reluctant board approval of a Collegiate Course for Women. Opposition remained strong: Professor John Howard Van Amringe, later to become dean of Columbia College, argued that "you can't teach a man mathematics if there's a girl in the room—and if you can, he isn't worth teaching." The course that was approved in 1883 was something of a joker: class attendance was forbidden, so the girls had to study elsewhere if they hoped to pass the examinations. Small wonder that few enrolled and that only eight girls ever succeeded in passing all the courses and securing degrees. President Barnard's hope for coeducation in Columbia College was never realized, but in 1889, the year of his death, a women's college was founded in New York and named after him. In 1900 Barnard College became a part of the University. Were President Barnard to return today, he would find nothing strange or unseemly in the presence on Columbia's campus of many young women in the uniform of the WAVES, and the sight of women students in all the graduate and professional schools would cheer him enormously.

Attaining the Heights

Columbia's second businessman-president was Barnard's successor in 1890. He was Seth Low of the class of 1870, who had already been mayor of Brooklyn and would later be mayor of New York. In his regime the trustees formally recognized Columbia's coming-of-age by changing the name from Columbia College to Columbia University. Physical growth, too, had to be accorded recognition and in 1897 Columbia moved once more.

SARTORIAL SPLENDOR AND THE
MAISON DE PUNK
The Class of 1881 at 49th Street

As the decade which we label the "gay nineties" opened,
the trustees began to look around for a home to replace
Columbia's outgrown campus at 49th Street. In 1891 they
decided upon the property which is the University's present
home on Morningside Heights, and which was then occupied by the Bloomingdale Asylum for the Insane. (After Columbia moved, one of the keepers at the Asylum stayed on
as a University guard and always referred to the students as

[11]

"the inmates.") In 1895 the cornerstone of the first building, Low Memorial Library, was laid. In 1896 the new site was dedicated, and in 1897 Columbia moved to 116th Street and Broadway. Morningside Heights, as the area was named in that year, attracted to it such institutions as the Cathedral of St. John the Divine, St. Luke's Hospital, and Union Theological Seminary. Before Union's arrival on the Heights, the College Tavern stood on the site and was the favorite rendezvous of more-or-less roistering Columbia students, although the Tavern did announce, "Freshmen not admitted unless accompanied by Upper Classmen."

The history of modern Columbia and the career of one man are synonymous. In 1901 young, handsome Nicholas Murray Butler of the class of 1882 succeeded Low as President, and President Barnard's dreams were to be more than fulfilled. In the four decades of Dr. Butler's presidency Columbia has become not only one of the largest universities in the world, but also one of the most unified and complete. Teachers College, of which Dr. Butler was first president, became part of Columbia in 1898. Today Columbia includes three colleges of liberal arts: Columbia College for men, Barnard College for women, and, at Annandale-on-Hudson, Bard College for men, founded in 1860 as St. Stephen's and renamed in recent years for the family of Dr. Samuel Bard of the class of 1763, pioneer in American medicine.

Graduate and professional schools at the Heights include:
The Graduate Faculties, which began with the School of Political Science in 1880, and now include the Faculty of Philosophy (1890) and the Faculty of Pure Science (1892). The present organization dates from 1909.

The School of Law, which began in 1858, although law lectures had been given as early as 1793 by James Kent.

WHEN FOOTBALL WAS A RUGGED GAME
Columbia vs. Princeton, 1890

The School of Engineering descends from the School of Mines (1864). In 1896 the ancestor was split into three separate schools, Mines, Engineering, and Chemistry. They were combined in 1929.

The School of Architecture started as a department in the School of Mines in 1881, and after spending some time as a part of the Faculty of Fine Arts, became a separate school in 1914.

The School of Journalism, founded and endowed by Joseph Pulitzer of the *New York World* and opened in 1912.

The School of Library Service, founded in 1887 as the School of Library Economy, transferred after two years to Albany as the New York State Library School, and returned to Columbia in 1926.

The School of Business, first opened in 1916.

Then there is Columbia's contribution to adult education, University Extension, and its nationally known and attended Summer Sessions which began in 1900.

[14]

Farther uptown, at Broadway and 168th Street, stands the Columbia-Presbyterian Medical Center. Here are located the College of Physicians and Surgeons, which traces its ancestry to the King's College medical faculty of 1767; the School of Dental and Oral Surgery, founded in 1916; and the Presbyterian Hospital School of Nursing, founded in 1892, which became a department of the College of Physicians and Surgeons in 1935. Several affiliated hospitals and institutes complete the Medical Center. Downtown on West 68th Street is the School of Pharmacy, founded as an independent school in 1829 and united with Columbia in 1904, and still farther downtown the New York School of Social Work, organized in 1898 and affiliated with Columbia since 1940. The New York Post-Graduate Medical School and Hospital on Second Avenue has been affiliated with Columbia since 1931, while on the island of Puerto Rico is another affiliated institution, the School of Tropical Medicine of the University of Puerto Rico.

Columbia's physical plant on Morningside Heights is a planned and unified whole, yet interesting architectural variety exists. Low Memorial Library, the first building, is surmounted by a dome which is the largest ever built of solid masonry in America; next to it there still stands one of the original Bloomingdale Asylum buildings, small, red-brick Alumni House. The University Libraries, which include more than 1,500,000 volumes, have their administrative headquarters in South Hall, whose book stack, of fifteen air-conditioned tiers with room for 4,000,000 books, is the largest ever constructed as a single unit; a few blocks away stands Columbia's newest structure, Brander Matthews Hall, home of dramatic activities and containing a theater which seats exactly 299 persons. There is beautiful, restful St. Paul's Chapel; to the north stands Pupin Physics Laboratories with its twelve stories of classrooms and modern research laboratories. At the southeast corner of the campus is

[15]

fifteen-story John Jay Hall, home of almost all student activities, and dormitory, in peacetime, for nearly 500 students. John Jay went up in a year and a half, but over behind Low Library stands ferry-boatish University Hall, which, after almost half a century, is still unfinished.

Perhaps the most interesting single room in the University is the Trustees Room in Low Memorial Library. Its walls are paneled from floor to ceiling in Irish bog oak with Ionic pilasters. At the head of the long mahogany table is the chair of the president of the University, a chair which once belonged to Benjamin Franklin. In the fireplace of Caen stone is set the cornerstone of old King's College, laid in 1756. The iron crown over the fireplace is also preserved from the original College building, and is one of the few royal emblems which escaped destruction in the Revolution. A photograph of the Royal Charter of 1754 may be seen under glass behind a sliding panel in the wall at one end of the room. The original, engrossed on vellum, is one of the University's most cherished historical possessions and makes public appearances only on such special occasions as the visit of the King and Queen of England in 1939.

In all, there are seventy buildings on the Morningside campus, and the University is the owner of a number of apartment houses on Claremont Avenue and Riverside Drive, and also Butler Hall on 119th Street and the King's Crown Hotel on 116th Street. Up at the end of Manhattan Island, at West 218th Street and Broadway, are the twenty-eight acres of Baker Field, including the football stadium and the Edwin Gould Boathouse. Exclusive of the Medical Center, Columbia stands on about seventy-eight acres of New York City land. In addition, Camp Columbia, recreation and engineering field study center at Lakeside, Conn., covers about 585 acres.

Columbia has its own central heating and power plant in University Hall, the heat and power turned out there being the equivalent in output of the public utility system of a moderate-sized city. The operation of this plant, as well as the many other activities necessary to keep Columbia going physically—from mopping floors to repairing roofs—re-

GRIDIRON HEROES POSE FOR THEIR PUBLIC
The 1881 Varsity

MANY MORE BUILDINGS TO COME

The Campus in 1898

quires a separate Department of Buildings and Grounds, which was first organized in 1886 and has been progressively busier ever since.

The University also has a separate Purchasing Department which in the course of a year is called upon to secure about every kind of item imaginable, from pencils to rare chemicals. With one hand it buys $10,000 worth of paint and $93,000 worth of coal a year, while with the other it is busy purchasing skeletons which may cost anywhere from $75 to several thousand dollars.

To Columbia students and teachers, however, one of the most interesting and useful aspects of the physical plant is the winding, gloomy, stone-walled tunnel, a story underground, which links most of the Morningside buildings. Its official purpose is to permit access to the bewildering array of pipes and conduits that carry heat and power. Unofficially, it is a great convenience in bad weather—providing one doesn't get lost, or doesn't spend too much time searching for the mythical branch of the tunnel under Broadway which, so College freshmen are told, leads to the very heart of Barnard.

The Real Columbia

As extensive, as important, and as valuable as Columbia's buildings and equipment may be, they are still not the essence of the University. The life and spirit of the institution are centered in its administrative organization, in its teachers and officers, and in its students. What this life and spirit are today is partly the result of natural growth and the environment in which Columbia has lived; partly the result of the personalities, ideas, and ideals of the leaders who have guided Columbia through her nearly two centuries of life.

The greatest environmental factor in Columbia's life has been the simple fact of her location in New York City. Columbia's growth from physical and intellectual youth to

THE PRESIDENT OF THE UNIVERSITY
Nicholas Murray Butler

[20]

mature but modern middle age has paralleled that of New York City. The same factors which developed the little eighteenth-century colonial town into the giant metropolis of twentieth-century America have been instrumental in transforming the tiny college of old-fashioned arts into a huge center of learning where the arts, the sciences, and the practical affairs and problems of modern life are equally at home.

Columbia is now so much a part of the metropolis that it is difficult to conceive of a Columbia located elsewhere being anything like the institution it is. Yet debate is old and not yet dead as to whether Columbia's undergraduate schools, at least, would not be better off in a more secluded spot. There is much to be said for the academic peace and quiet of a rural campus with more wide open spaces, more trees, and fewer attractions and distractions to take one's mind off the immediate problem of preparing for tomorrow's classes. The debate, nevertheless, has been rather definitely resolved in favor of Columbia University *in the City of New York*. Street noises may sometimes blot out a few words of a lecture but undergraduate, graduate, and professional education turn out in the end, to one's satisfaction, to be composed of not just what teachers and books had to offer but also of the music, theater, art, business, finance, industry, politics, and amusements of New York.

Columbia, like the city and nation of which it is a part, is big: its teaching staff numbers more than 3,300; in peacetime its student body numbers more than 30,000; it thinks nothing of the fact that it has conferred at one commencement as many as 5,000 degrees and certificates; its capital aggregates $160,000,000; the total value of its land, buildings, and equipment is approximately $60,000,000; its annual budget runs in the neighborhood of $10,000,000. But Columbia's bigness is not the bigness of an untrained and undisciplined mob; it is the bigness of a well-trained and well-organized army where the success of the whole depends on the specialized skill and purpose of a variety of small units.

The many constituent parts of Columbia are smoothly unified in the larger organization. At the top are the twenty-four trustees—six of whom are elected upon nomination of the alumni—in whom is vested the title to all corporate property and who exercise the power of appointment to all offices and general oversight of University affairs. Academic plans and policies are guided and supervised by the University Council, headed by the president of the University and consisting of the deans and directors of the several schools and faculties, as well as other delegates chosen by and from those bodies. But within the schools and faculties a large measure of self-rule exists, not merely in theory but in practice. Most of these component parts are small—Columbia College before the war, for example, never accepted more than approximately 1,700 students; Journalism and Architecture, sixty or seventy each—and contact between teacher and student has, throughout Columbia's long history, been close and frequent.

While modern Columbia owes the general shape of its policies and its steady progress along many specific lines to the genius and energy of one man, Nicholas Murray Butler, Dr. Butler himself is the first to give credit to the very great number of deans, administrators, and teachers who have kept Columbia in the van of educational thought and action. Out of a course on the origins and meaning of World War I, for example, came in 1919 the Columbia College course now known as Contemporary Civilization, which in one form or another has spread all over the country wherever colleges and universities have recognized the need for presenting a synthesizing background to the complex economic, social, political, and moral problems of our western civilization. There is much talk today of a college education based on the reading of "great books." Not so long after his graduation in 1900, the later nationally known author John Erskine conceived and taught a course that utilized fundamentally the same idea.

Columbia's growth has not been within itself only. More and more it has recognized and taken its place in the life of the nation. Its faculty members, long before the Roosevelt administration made "Brain Trusts" famous, were consulted by business and government on many problems. Literally hundreds of them have made significant contributions to the physical sciences, to the arts and humanities, and to the social sciences.

Throughout the years Columbia has been able to take pride in the eminence and public service of many of its alumni. Alexander Hamilton and John Jay have already been mentioned, but the University is also glad that it can claim Clement Clarke Moore, class of 1798, who wrote the imperishable " 'Twas the Night before Christmas." Six Columbia men were members of the Continental Congress; Washington had two in his cabinet. All but one of the committee on style which put the finishing touches on the Constitution of the United States were connected with Columbia. Gouverneur Morris, 1768, put all future Americans in his debt by securing a decimal system of currency for this country. Robert R. Livingston, 1765, while U. S. Minister to France, secured the greatest real estate bargain in our history when he bought the vast territory of Louisiana from Napoleon in 1803.

President Theodore Roosevelt and President Franklin D. Roosevelt followed almost identical educational paths. Both received their undergraduate education at Harvard; both entered the Columbia Law School, the former with the class of 1882, the latter with the class of 1907. Many other Columbians are active in government and politics, including New York's Governor Thomas E. Dewey, 1925 Law. Both the present Chief Justice of the Supreme Court, Harlan Fiske Stone, 1898, and his predecessor, Charles Evans Hughes,

ROYALTY ASCENDS THE LIBRARY STEPS

King George and Queen Elizabeth, 1939

[24]

1884, received their professional training in the Columbia School of Law. Two other present-day justices, Stanley F. Reed, 1909, and William O. Douglas, 1925, are Law School alumni, and the late philosopher and jurist, Benjamin N. Cardoza, received his training at Columbia.

Two Columbians who not only achieved success in their own fields but who also typify the life and spirit of America are Lou Gehrig, 1925 College, and Paul Robeson, 1923 Law. Students have come to Columbia from other countries and have returned home to become leaders. Among such alumni are V. K. Wellington Koo, 1909 College, and Hu Shih, 1927 Ph.D., both diplomatic representatives of modern China. Among the graduates of Columbia are men and women who have made outstanding careers in every walk of life. There are authors, publishers, editors, and foreign correspondents; lawyers and judges; clergymen and educators; engineers and industrialists; businessmen and financiers; physicians and surgeons.

Outside the Classroom

Columbia's history and her modern life are not concerned with academic matters alone. Social life, student activities, and athletics have played an increasingly important part as in all American colleges. The oldest surviving tradition of this aspect of Columbia's history is represented by the Philolexian Society, founded in 1802. As early as 1766, however, a literary society was founded and it became customary for each senior class to establish its own Senior Society for Literary Improvement. Philolexian, or "Philo" as it has been better known for many, many years, had a rival after 1806 when Peithologian was founded and formal joint debates began between the societies.

Another custom began in 1863 when the first of the Goodwood cups was awarded by vote to the most popular junior. This went on for fifteen years, the trophy being ranked as the highest undergraduate honor and the occasion of its award being accompanied by a speech and a celebration. A colorful ceremony was originated by the class of 1862 and lasted, in one form or another, until 1914. This was the *Perideipnon,* or "funeral feast," a celebration at the end of the sophomore year at which certain unpopular textbooks were burned. The sophomores wore black gowns, with skull and crossbones, and paraded bearing torches. Unpopular professors could count on being burned in effigy. Generally the president of the College would respond to calls for a speech, after which the parade always managed to wind up at Fritz's Café, conveniently located in the backyard of a nearby brewery.

OFF FOR A GAIN, HE HOPES

Action on Baker Field

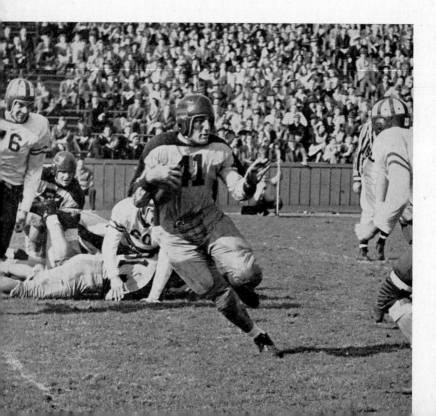

Other ceremonies, such as Class Day which was initiated in 1865, did not differ much from their counterparts of today. There were the Senior Ball, the Junior Reception, freshman rushes, and, of course, Commencement. The Commencement ceremony has been held in many different places, but not until the removal to Morningside Heights were outdoor ceremonies attempted. Now, weather permitting, South Court and South Field in front of Low Library are converted into an enormous amphitheater where as many as 20,000 visitors come to see the always colorful academic procession and the awarding of degrees, and to hear the annual Commencement address of the president.

Columbia students undertook their initial venture in publishing in 1815 when Peithologian launched (and the same year abandoned) *Academic Recreations,* the first printed publication. After that there was no student publication until 1848 when the senior class issued a sixteen-page catalogue of the College, containing the names of trustees, faculty, and students. This venture was continued regularly by the seniors as a college yearbook until 1858, when the trustees decided to take over its publication. Seven years passed without further student publishing. Then the junior class began a purely student annual, *Columbian.* The name was changed to *Columbiad* the next year but in 1890, when *The Miner* was merged with it, it went back to *Columbian* and has so remained ever since.

The first real student newspaper was launched in 1867 with the title of *Cap and Gown.* This publication united the functions of a literary journal with those of a newspaper. It appeared monthly until 1877, changing its name in 1873 to *Acta Columbiana.* In 1877 some former editors of the *Acta* founded the *Spectator,* a fortnightly which soon became distinctive for its cartoons, and which in 1885 absorbed the *Acta.* The *Spectator* continued to grow until in 1902 it reached the stature of a five-times-a-week morning paper. It remained a daily paper until depression and war took their toll, and still continues publishing despite difficulties.

Spectator gave up its literary functions in 1892, turning them over to the *Literary Monthly* which, after various changes of name, ended up as the *Columbia Review*. *Jester*, the College comic, although not boasting as long a history, appropriately picked All Fools' Day, 1901, to launch itself. As a wartime measure these two publications have recently combined as the *Jester Review*.

Early musical efforts at Columbia usually took the form of class quartets, although the first Glee Club was organized sixty years ago. Today students participate not only in the Glee Club, but also the Chapel Choir, an orchestra, and two bands, marching and symphonic, all with the professional aid of the Music Department.

The theater, too, has had and continues to have its devotees among students. Best known is Varsity Show, a musical comedy written and acted by students, with the feminine roles played by men, including a pony ballet which, with its football heavyweights, has upon occasion almost literally brought down the house. Top dramatic group at Columbia is the Columbia Theater Associates, through which individual units produce in the course of a year a variety of theatrical offerings, old and new, serious and comic, with and without music.

The newest member of the activities family is the Radio Club which installed and operates CURC, a "wired wireless" broadcasting station of the kind which has recently enjoyed great popularity on many campuses.

The home and heart of undergraduate extracurricular activities is the fourth floor of John Jay Hall. The "head office" of the nonathletic activities is King's Crown, a department of the University coördinating what were, until the war, a wide variety of activities in which hundreds of students participated each year. Participation is, of course, voluntary and subject only to the maintenance of proper academic standing. Self-government is the rule in all activities, within the bounds of good taste and common sense, both in editorial and in business affairs. Highly-prized gold and silver crowns in the form of charms are awarded for service and excellence in these activities. The musical, literary, and dramatic activities have been curtailed since war came, but neither the University nor its alumni and students doubt that they will become vigorous again when peace comes.

Student self-government in the College is effected through the Board of Student Representatives, chosen by popular vote. A chapter of Phi Beta Kappa, scholastic honorary society, was established at the University in 1869. Nacoms, founded in 1898, is a secret honorary society which each year selects for membership fifteen outstanding juniors of Columbia College. A similar society, Sachems, was started in 1915. There are many other organizations, clubs, and societies throughout the University, each with its special purpose, each with its group of interested students.

Greek-letter fraternities, of which there were thirteen in 1881, have played an important part in the social life of Columbia, their number and influence fluctuating with the times. In the years immediately preceding World War II those fraternities which had weathered the economic troubles of the early thirties formed a new interfraternity association, Pamphratria, inaugurating an era of real coöperation.

Today all religious activities, which once were carried on by the Columbia University Christian Association, are included in the organization of the University. Working with the chaplain of the University are three religious advisers, one Protestant, one Catholic, and one Jewish. Not only are the interests of members of the different faiths provided for through these offices, but in addition there is much practical and heartening interfaith activity.

Organized athletics did not exist until after Columbia moved to 49th Street. The class of 1859 took up crew, and eight years later a baseball association was formed. It was in baseball that the first intercollegiate competitions took place, Yale's team coming to New York in May, 1868, to meet the Columbians. Franklin Bryant Torrey of the class of 1881 is credited with being the first individual to pitch a curved ball. In 1869 college contests in track were first held.

Two great crew victories in the seventies brought Columbia wide athletic fame: in the second intercollegiate regatta at Saratoga in 1874; and at Henley, England, in 1878, in which the four-man Columbia crew won the Visitor's Cup by defeating both Oxford and Cambridge. In the Saratoga victory Columbia outrowed Wesleyan, Harvard, Williams, Dartmouth, Cornell, Trinity, Princeton, and Yale and set a record over a three-mile course on slack water which stood for more than twenty-five years. In 1895 the Intercollegiate Rowing Association established its annual classic on the Hudson at Poughkeepsie, and Columbia has been a regular competitor.

For the Columbians of yesterday there were, besides baseball and rowing, tennis, cricket, lacrosse, and cycling. The classes from 1869 to 1872 had their Velocipede Club, which reappeared in 1879 as the Bicycle Club.

The class of 1865 was the first to try out the new-fangled game of football, using a convenient field east of Fifth Avenue and 50th Street. In 1870 Rutgers challenged Columbia, and, perhaps with the advantage of being one of the American pioneers of the sport, defeated the New Yorkers 6 to 3 in the fourth college game played in the United States. There were twenty men to a team then, as there still were in 1872 when Yale had as its first intercollegiate football opponent the gridiron representatives of Columbia. Yale, so Columbians like to think, had beginners' luck, coming out ahead 3 to 0.

In 1880 the Columbia College Football Association was formed, and the same year Columbia was admitted to the Intercollegiate Football Association, the other members of which were Yale, Harvard, and Princeton. Columbia did not have a football team every year, and in 1905 football was formally abolished, not to be revived for ten years. Thereupon the first team of the new era went through its season undefeated. The most recent phase of Columbia football is the Lou Little era which began in 1930, and whose high point is, and in the minds of Columbia adherents will always remain, the 7–0 Rose Bowl victory over Stanford on New Year's Day, 1934.

Until Columbia moved to its present home, its athletes seldom had a field they could call their own. The two square blocks from 114th to 116th Streets, between Broadway and Amsterdam Avenue, were acquired in 1903, and as South Field the entire plot was for a time devoted to an athletic field. Even without the gradual encroachment of Hamilton, Hartley, Furnald, Livingston, Journalism, John Jay, and South Halls, with the increasing interest in athletics South Field became inadequate as a varsity sports arena. For a while, beginning in 1906, the problem seemed solved when the state gave Columbia the privilege of building a stadium out into the Hudson River between 116th and 120th Streets. Drawings of the proposed structure still exist, but the prohibitive cost killed the venture in the planning stage.

It was not until 1922 that Columbia came into possession of ample athletic facilities, through the generosity of banker George Fisher Baker, whose gift of the "Dyckman tract" at the very northern end of Manhattan Island cost him $825,000 in all. Today Baker Field is a modern athletic plant with facilities for crew and track, as well as varsity football and baseball fields. The Dyckman Manor House, now a club-house and training quarters, is a commodious wooden residence which stood on the plot when Columbia took over.

A large bronze statue of the Columbia Lion, athletic mascot, is mounted on a granite pedestal and occupies a rocky pinnacle overlooking the practice field. It was presented by the class of 1899. The Lion as emblem of Columbia was adopted by the Board of Student Representatives in 1910, following the presentation of a blue and white banner, bearing a lion rampant, with the motto *Leo Columbiae*. The banner was the gift of the Society of the Early Eighties, one of Columbia's most loyal and generous alumni organizations. The need for college colors was felt long ago, and the present combination of light blue and white was adopted as early as 1852. The light blue was taken from the Philolexian and the white from the Peithologian society.

Varsity competition is—or was until the war put such things on something like a day-to-day basis—in football, baseball, basketball, track, crew, cross-country, swimming, water polo, wrestling, fencing, and tennis. An extensive and growing program of intramural sports brings hundreds of students into activity and competition each year.

Alumni Organizations

For several years a friendly argument was carried on between Columbia and Williams College as to which institution was entitled to the honor of claiming the oldest alumni

OUT FOR PRACTICE
A Recent Columbia Crew

organization in the country. That debate now seems resolved by the finding of a yellowed volume among Columbia's old records. Williams may still claim the oldest continuously functioning alumni group, founded in 1820, but Columbia now has the evidence to show that its graduates first got together in a formal manner on December 21, 1815. Those early alumni, who organized as The Literary Institution of Columbia College, met regularly for two years, "reading papers on literary and scientific subjects," and discussing such matters as "The Prospects of the Bourbons," and "The Probable Duration of the Constitution of the United States." They obtained the use of a room in the College building at Park Place, which they fitted up in an "elegant manner."

In 1825 the Association of the Alumni of Columbia College was founded, and today is an active and important part of the University's life. Its objects at first were both social and cultural, and it led an active life until 1844 when, as is so often the case with such organizations, it went into a period of decline. Revived in 1856, it has carried on its activities without a break. In 1858 it established the Alumni Prize, one of the oldest awards of its kind in American collegiate circles. Every year since then this prize has been presented, by vote of his classmates, to the "most faithful and deserving student of the graduating class."

As Columbia College became Columbia University, other alumni groups representing the various schools took their places with the College Association. In 1859 the Association of the Alumni of the College of Physicians and Surgeons was founded; in 1860 the Alumni Association of the Law School; in 1872 the Engineering Schools Alumni Association. The logical outcome of the growth of the University and its alumni bodies was realized in 1913 when the Alumni Federation of Columbia University came into being. Organized, as its name implies, on a basis similar to that of our national government, it brings together the nine different alumni associations now active. Besides the older groups, these are: Alumni Association of the School of Architecture, Alumni Association of the Graduate Schools, Association of Dental Alumni, Alumni Association of the School of Journalism, and Alumni Association of the School of Business. Barnard College, Teachers College, and the School of Library Service each has an alumni organization of its own.

The Federation, through its permanent staff in Alumni House, carries on many activities and services: for the more than 100,000 living graduates of the University it keeps records, arranges dinners and luncheons, manages the Alumni Fund, and publishes the *Columbia Alumni News*.

There is, in addition, the Columbia University Club, with a large clubhouse in midtown Manhattan. Founded in 1901 and located in various other homes before settling down in its present location in 1917, the Club had as its first president the late, unforgettable Dean John Howard Van Amringe, of the College, loyal and enthusiastic alumnus, long-time teacher of mathematics, whose memory Columbia men have perpetuated in song and stone, notably in the Van Am Quadrangle on the College campus.

THE ORIGINAL KING'S CROWN
A Momento of Park Place

II. UNIVERSITY IN UNIFORM

The First Five Wars

THE Revolution remains the only one of the nation's wars which has forced Columbia to close its doors. Not until World War I did armed conflict have an impact on the University approaching that of the country's first struggle.

Students and alumni have, of course, put on uniform and fought for their country in every conflict. Response to the outbreak of the Revolution on the part of both students and graduates was immediate, but not one-sided, and those who fought seem to have been about evenly divided between Tory and Rebel. On the side of the patriots was young Alexander Hamilton, whose fateful path to fame led to his service as lieutenant colonel and aide-de-camp to Washington, as first Secretary of the Treasury, as co-author with John Jay and James Madison of the *Federalist,* and, finally, to his death in a duel with Aaron Burr. Prominent on the side of the Loyalists was another King's College man, Sir Samuel Auchmuty, G.C.B., who rose to the rank of lieutenant general in the British Army. In the same month of September, 1776, that saw the College forced to give up its work for the duration, a battle was fought on Manhattan Island, on a spot then far north of the city limits—the Battle of Harlem Heights. This battlefield, as it turned out many years later, was to become Columbia University's present home on Morningside Heights.

During the War of 1812 the students of Columbia College were dismissed from their classes for several days so that they could go up to McGowan's Pass, about where 123d Street is now, and not far from the present campus, to help build fortifications. A Columbia uncle and nephew are prominent in the annals of two wars: Stephen Watts Kearny, class of 1812, was a brigadier general in the Mexican War; his nephew, the dashing Philip Kearny, class of 1833, fought in both the Mexican and Civil Wars. In the former he held the rank of major; in the latter he rose to be major general in 1862 and that same year was killed at the Battle of Chantilly in Virginia.

The Civil War in its effects on Columbia followed much the same pattern as had the nation's previous wars. Many students and alumni enlisted, and a number of Columbians were killed or died in the service of the Union. President King's son Augustus, of the class of 1860, was one of these. An impressive number of graduates of the College of Physicians and Surgeons served as Army doctors in the great conflict. At the first war Commencement some of the students present were already in the uniform of the Seventh and Seventy-First Regiments. Students who remained in college met in a loft on Sixth Avenue near Eighth Street and were drilled by a former Army sergeant. On April 10, 1865, President Barnard announced General Lee's surrender and declared a holiday. The Columbia students thereupon marched down to Washington Square to see that New York University had a holiday too.

A bronze tablet in Hamilton Hall keeps alive the memory of Sergeant Hamilton Fish, Jr., of the First United States Volunteer Cavalry, who was the first American soldier to die in action in the Spanish-American War. Fish, class of 1895, was the grandson of the great Hamilton Fish, class of 1827, who was Secretary of State throughout President Grant's administration.

Until World War I, Columbia's fighting men for the most

[37]

PARADE ON 116TH STREET
The Columbia Battalion, 1917

part made their names known on land rather than at sea, although there was a member of the class of 1858 who was destined to achieve as much naval renown as any American. He was Alfred T. Mahan, later Admiral Mahan and author of the classic, *The Influence of Sea Power upon History, 1660–1783*. Admiral Mahan spent two years at Columbia as an undergraduate before going to Annapolis, and in 1900 he returned to the campus to receive an honorary degree.

World War I

One who today turns back the pages of Columbia's history to the chapter on World War I is surprised, not at the great difference between 1917–18 and 1941–44, but at the striking similarity in the pattern of events. Almost everything going on at Columbia today had its counterpart on the campus of a quarter century ago.

As early as May, 1916, a University mass meeting was held to pledge support to what was then called preparedness, rather than rearmament. That summer more than 500 Columbia students and alumni went to Plattsburg for voluntary military training. Many others, inclined to the Navy rather than the Army, took a training cruise. Thirty Columbia men were aboard the USS *Maine* and a Columbian on another ship sent back to the campus a snapshot showing, among other ships in the force he was with, the USS *Illinois* which in the next war, as the USS *Prairie State,* was to be intimately connected with the University as part of the Midshipmen's School.

In this pre-war period Columbia men were also active in rélief and hospital work abroad. Robert Arrowsmith, class of 1882, was in Europe as a representative of the Commission for Relief in Belgium, while Elbridge Colby, class of 1912, sailed as head of the Columbia Serbian Relief Expedition which included twenty-five other Columbians.

On February 6, 1917, the gymnasium was filled with students and faculty members gathered together in an official University assembly. The occasion was the severance of diplomatic relations with Germany, and President Butler and other speakers put the University on record as supporting the action. Within a month a committee on national defense, similar to the committee which was to be named a quarter of a century later under almost identical circumstances, was announced. With it there appeared a complete plan for the organization of the University for national service. This plan contemplated three initial steps: (1) the compilation of a personnel index of faculty, students, and alumni; (2) the organization of the University internally so as to render the most effective service; and (3) the establishment of relations with the proper government departments. Later the

[39]

Bureau of Education of the Department of the Interior recommended the Columbia plan in its entirety to all the colleges and universities of the country.

The first direct military activity on the campus also began a month before the United States entered the war. One thousand undergraduates met on March 8 to form the Columbia Reserve Officers Training Corps, usually referred to as the Columbia Battalion or the Columbia Corps. This unit began drilling at once and at the same time a naval unit began learning about sea warfare on the USS *Granite State,* moored in the Hudson at 97th Street. By April 27, three weeks after war came, the Columbia Battalion was able to hold its first official parade, and on May 6 a special farewell service for the many students who were about to enter the Army was preceded by a review on South Field at which the Battalion's "right-about-face while at double quick . . . brought a storm of applause from the crowd." Within four months of its start, 1,400 men had enrolled in the Battalion and nearly 300 of them had gone on to Plattsburg or into some National Guard unit. That summer 300 Columbians were at Plattsburg, a larger number than from any other eastern university.

The Battalion was placed on a more formal basis in the fall of 1917 when Lieutenant, later Captain, Ralph Hodder-Williams, wounded veteran of Princess Patricia's Canadian Light Infantry and holder of the Victoria Cross, was engaged by the University as commanding officer. The Battalion became a regular course of four hours drill a week, with credit given to the students who participated. There were about 300 men in the Battalion at this time, and although they had only wooden rifles, the course was thorough and intensive.

In the spring of 1918 the entire Battalion took part in a Liberty Loan parade and marched all the way from Washington Square to the Morningside Campus. This was almost the last official function of the Battalion, for in April, 1918, it was announced that at the request of the University a Reserve Officers' Training Corps would be established at the opening of the next academic year. Military training was to become compulsory for all students in the College, and Colonel John P. Finley was detailed as professor of military science and tactics.

Columbia did not get its R.O.T.C. unit, however, for in the late summer of 1918 the Army announced a new plan for training men to be officers. Columbia, said President Butler in announcing the University's participation, would henceforth be, for practical purposes, divided into two parts. One would be under military organization and command and was to consist of the Students' Army Training Corps, which would comprise the male students in all schools of the University who were classed as available for military service. At the induction ceremony on October 1 more than 2,000 men lined up in formation, but they had not yet been put in uniform.

CEREMONY ON 116TH STREET
The Columbia S.A.T.C., 1918

VISITORS FROM FRANCE
Statesman Viviani and Marshal Joffre, 1917

The S.A.T.C., including a naval unit, was housed in Hartley and Livingston halls, much as the V-12 seamen are today. There were, however, four cots to a room, and other quarters, such as the Home for the Blind and Aged at 104th Street and Broadway, the Speyer School on 120th Street, and a garage on 124th Street, were taken over. Officers were quartered in fraternity houses and other buildings, and the headquarters of the Corps was established in Journalism. Major Herbert C. Earnshaw shortly succeeded Colonel Finley as commanding officer, while Rear Admiral Joseph K. Taussig was "skipper" of the naval contingent. The members of the Corps followed Army routine. They were up at 6 A. M., had calisthenics, and messed in University Hall. Lights went out at 10 P. M. and guards were constantly on duty as they are today, the only difference being in the uniforms. The Corps even took over the student newspaper, which became the *Columbia S.A.T.C. Spectator.*

The curriculum devised by Columbia for the S.A.T.C. was adopted as a model for other colleges by the War Department and one course in particular, "Issues of the War," was used by all S.A.T.C. units in the country.

A first group of sixty men left the Corps for officers' training camp in October, but the Corps as a whole hardly had an opportunity to get organized before the war ended. The Corps held an Armistice Day parade and it is recorded that the Barnard College girls fell in behind, four abreast. By early December, Columbia's S.A.T.C. had its orders to disband.

The two summers of 1917 and 1918 had not been complete gaps in the military training offered at Columbia. In May, 1917, plans were prepared for using Camp Columbia, in Connecticut, for a special course for those students of Columbia and other schools who were too young or were otherwise ineligible to go to a government camp. Fifty-eight students attended the camp in 1917, building their own rifle range and digging 400 yards of trenches. The course, besides drill, included mapping and the construction of military roads, bridges, and trenches. The camp was in charge of Captain Hodder-Williams, with Professor James Kip Finch as resident director. The camp course was repeated in the summer of 1918, with about twice as many in attendance.

While Army uniforms predominated on the campus in 1917–18 in much the same way that Navy uniforms do today, there was considerable Navy activity also. Before war was declared a Motor Boat Patrol Unit was formed. Fifty-four motor boats were offered by alumni for the use of the unit and the Association of Doctors of Philosophy presented a complete set of signal flags. Later that spring sixty naval reserve officers took a three weeks course at Columbia. Of them the Alumni News reported: "They are all watermen, many of them captains and pilots of deep sea merchant vessels, with a large representation of wealthy yachtsmen of the college type." Besides navigation and signaling, they were "instructed in artillery with the rapid fire and automatic type of gun."

In March, 1917, sixteen College students had asked Professor Lincoln de G. Moss, a naval veteran of the Spanish-American War, to instruct them for service in the Navy. This instruction ran for ten weeks and was so successful that it was then federalized. By September, 300 officers and men were on campus as the Naval Reserve Instruction School. Part of the course had to do with gas engines; this phase of the work took on such importance that it was expanded and soon became the separate U. S. Navy Gas Engine School. Professor Charles E. Lucke, 1902 Ph.D., was civilian director. To meet the U-boat menace, large numbers of submarine chasers were being built. They were equipped with engines of a type different from that on any other ships in the Navy, and, consequently, there was an immediate need for men with special training to handle them.

THEIR SECOND DAY ON THE CAMPUS
The First Columbia Midshipmen, 1942

The Gas Engine School in the fall of 1917 was prepared to take in a class of sixty men every two weeks. For the four-week course, one of the Columbia laboratories was fitted out like a sub-chaser. In the last six months of 1917 the school trained 700 men and at the beginning of 1918 it was announced that "the first class of men to be trained to care for engines of Navy flying machines" would arrive in a few days. Professor Lucke was commissioned a lieutenant commander; later, in recognition of the important work so successfully performed by the school, the Navy broke one of its long-standing rules and promoted him to commander.

In early 1918, the U. S. Signal Corps Radio School made its appearance on the campus. Its 150 students were to be trained "to care for the wireless used on airplanes and otherwise in connection with aviation," and when the school was publicly announced it "satisfied considerable campus curiosity, concerning three airplanes which had been hauled onto the University grounds."

Columbia's College of Physicians and Surgeons was active many months before the United States entered the war. By the end of 1916, for example, twenty-two members of the staff, fifteen students, and a number of alumni had rendered medical service in Europe. A few months later the College was enrolling doctors and dentists for service if called by the armed forces and a base hospital was in process of organization. On May 14, 1917, Base Hospital Unit Number Two of the Presbyterian Hospital sailed for Europe, the first New York unit of its kind to leave for the front. Many Columbia men sailed with it.

Early in April, 1917, the University trustees had approved plans for the erection of the Columbia War Hospital on a tract of land known as the Columbia Oval in the Bronx. Almost as soon as the plan was announced, $50,000 was subscribed by the public and facilities for 500 patients were ready in a short time. Air raids were not a threatening menace in World War I, but there was some fear of naval bombardment of New York and the hospital was intended to handle, if necessary, victims of such bombardment or of other war disasters, as well as ill soldiers. On October 3, 1917, the War Department took over the fully equipped hospital which then became known as U. S. Army General Hospital Number One—the first put into service after war started. For a time it was used as temporary quarters for doctors and nurses who were about to go overseas.

In the course of the war Columbia made various other contributions to the nation's work. In April, 1917, more than 125 alumni and students became interested in the Aerial Coast Patrol and were formed into Patrol Unit Number

Four. Shortly they were "contemplating the purchase of Howard S. Borden's seaplane" as "the unit has no machine at present." They needed $8,000 to buy the plane. As soon as war was declared, Teachers College announced plans to instruct qualified chefs in a course which would enable them in turn to teach Army cooks. The University Library, in a preview of the Victory Book Campaign of World War II, was helping collect books—with the slogan which is again being used, "Our boys want books."

Early in 1918 the Army established a School of Military Cinematography. Before the end of 1917 the School of Pharmacy had trained 300 men for the Naval Hospital Corps. An Army Ordnance School, with seventy-five students at a time taking a six-weeks course, began in early 1918 to train men to handle the technical stores and to perform the accounting duties of the Ordnance Field Service. In the fall of 1918, at the request of the War and Navy Departments, the School of Engineering opened an emergency course for students entering from high school, foreshadowing in some respects the V-12 Navy College Program and the Army Specialized Training Program of today.

By September, 1917, Columbia alumni had raised enough money to supply all the ambulances and other equipment for an entire Ambulance Service Division. One class alone, that of 1894, had sent six ambulances, and it was claimed that Columbia had given more ambulances than any other college. Shortly after the American University Union was established in Paris, a Columbia Service Bureau became part of the Union. Under the direction of Horatio S. Krans, of the class of 1894, the Bureau was a friendly and helpful port of call for hundreds of Columbia soldiers on leave in Paris. Back home on the campus the University inaugurated the Columbia War Papers as a contribution to the solution of various nonmilitary problems arising out of the war. The first of these found philosopher John Dewey writing on what

WEEKLY EVENT ON SOUTH FIELD
The Midshipmen Pass in Review

we today call Victory Gardens. In all 150,000 copies of these pamphlets were distributed. About the same time the *Alumni News* began issuing military supplements, the first being "Notes on Field Service Regulations."

The war records kept by the Alumni office show that approximately 7,500 students and alumni went into government service, most of them in the armed forces. At least 150 are known to have been killed in action or to have died while in the service of their country.

In the period of the war and the years immediately following, Columbia was host to a greater number of famous personages than at any other time in her history. Honorary degrees were conferred on Marshal Joseph Jacques Césaire

Joffre, René Viviani, Arthur James Balfour, Robert Lansing, King Albert of Belgium, Herbert C. Hoover, General John J. Pershing, Désiré Joseph Cardinal Mercier, Aristide Briand, and Marshal Ferdinand Foch.

For Columbia, World War I was a period of great activity of a nature the campus had never before known. The University met the test and gave its best to the nation, hoping—in vain, as it has turned out—that history would not, for once, have to repeat itself.

The University Enlists Again

June, 1940: the Low Countries had been overrun; France was falling and Dunkirk was about to stun not only England but the entire anti-Axis world. More Americans began to show more interest in and concern for the state of the nation's defenses. In Washington the government moved to increase and speed up the rearmament program.

In that same month, when there still were Americans who refused to believe that the war could ever involve this country, Columbia University took its first public and official steps toward contributing its resources to the nation's defense. President Butler appointed a University Committee on National Defense which at once set about examining the ways in which Columbia could help and which established relations with appropriate agencies and departments in Washington. In September, as a new academic year was about to start, the committee issued its first bulletin to several thousand students, setting forth the opportunities open to them in the growing defense program. In that bulletin the committee stated in unequivocal language the University's position—stating it, it should be noted, at a time when the "isolationist-interventionist" debate had not yet been settled by the march of events:

"True to its history, its traditions, and its ideals Columbia will do everything in its power to coöperate with the govern-

ment and with other organized agencies to protect and defend those fundamental principles of American economic, social, and political life which are so dear to us and which have made so profound an impression upon the thought of the world. At the moment, these fundamental principles are quite obviously in danger, and our task is, in accordance with our traditions and ideals, to coöperate in every possible way for their protection and defense."

Also in June, 1940, the Alumni Federation set up its own Committee on National Defense to act as a clearing house of information and assistance between the University and the alumni and between the government and the alumni. From the starting point marked by the organization of these two committees, the University's war work began and continued to spread into many fields in the next three years. More than a year before Pearl Harbor the "paper work" necessary to get General Hospital Number Two ready to go into uniform was completed at Columbia's College of Physicians and Surgeons. The Hospital has now been on active duty for many months. Evacuation Hospital Number Seven was formed at the New York Post-Graduate Medical School and Hospital and has also been on active duty for some time.

By the fall of 1940 Columbia had established a unit for training pilots under the Civil Aeronautics Authority, and in the School of Engineering an orientation course in military engineering and surveying was being given. In that same school courses shortly began under the Engineering, Science and Management Defense Training Program of the U. S. Office of Education. University Extension, in the fall of 1940, offered new courses growing out of interest in the war and in national preparedness. Intensive language courses (in Japanese, for one) were another University contribution, and

ROW ON ROW OF NAVY BLUE
The Midshipmen in Formation

the only course in the country in Albanian was begun. Faculty members and alumni in increasing numbers entered the armed services or joined the staffs of civilian war agencies. To the Army, for example, went Chemistry Professor J. Enrique Zanetti who, as Colonel Zanetti, is the Army's leading authority on incendiary bombs. To the Navy went Dean Joseph W. Barker of Engineering as special assistant to Secretary Knox.

Probably no school of the University has been involved in the war in more different ways than has Engineering. In fact, the war is directly responsible for its giving up the dubious distinction of being the only Columbia school not open to women: in October, 1942, a special engineering course for women was offered. The school has even given a course popularly known as "Lipstick 13." Actually it was a very serious course for women engineering aides, training them for work with the Grumman Aircraft Engineering Corporation.

As war approached and then became a reality, a new phrase was heard increasingly on college campuses throughout the country. The phrase was "accelerated programs," which, when translated into action, meant unusual, and sometimes bewildering, changes in the calendar of the University. Students began entering on dates which never had witnessed such a procedure before. It became difficult, if not impossible, for a student to tell to just which class he belonged. In 1942 to help meet the national emergency, Columbia College admitted freshmen in February, for the first time in a decade, and in July for the first time in history a freshman class began its work in the summer. This enabled students to secure at least part of their college education before being called in the draft, and, at the same time, to prepare themselves for more useful service in the Army and Navy.

The College now has three regular sessions per year for

civilian students, instead of the traditional two. Students in the College and in the School of Engineering may now obtain their degrees in two years and eight months instead of the customary four years, the first new classes under this program having been admitted in June, 1942. In neither case, though, does this mean that the quantity or quality of the education offered has been cut down. So far as possible all important features have been retained in spite of the growing demands on the schools' time and facilities for training men in uniform.

The College of Physicians and Surgeons and the School of Dental and Oral Surgery began, in the summer of 1942, a compulsory schedule of four quarterly terms per year. Barnard College, Bard College, and the School of Law also "accelerated" their programs. In the latter school the usual three year course can be completed in two years.

THE MIDSHIPMEN MARCH, THE BAND PLAYS
Honor Men Review the Regiment

The College of Pharmacy offered an "accelerated" program for seniors in the summer of 1942, and a year later provided a speeded-up schedule for sophomores and juniors also. The school is now operating on the basis of three sixteen-week sessions per year, permitting graduation in two years and eight months. The school is also the only pharmacy college in the country selected by the Coast Guard for training hospital corpsmen. In May, 1942, within two weeks of receiving a proposal from the Coast Guard, a twelve-week program was in operation and the first class of 200 men was assigned. The sixth and last class entered in the fall of 1943. Although the course does not qualify the men for licensure as civilian pharmacists, it has provided approximately 1,200 efficient and badly needed pharmacist's mates for the Coast Guard. That the course is a stiff and concentrated one may be judged from the list of subjects studied: anatomy, physiology, first aid and minor surgery, chemistry, pharmacy, materia medica, bacteriology, hematology, hygiene and sanitation, toxicology, arithmetic, nursing, diets and messing for the sick, and clerical procedure.

While Columbia was shifting its schedule to a wartime basis and performing the various services noted above, many students, with the guidance and coöperation of the University, were beginning their transition from civilian life to service in the armed forces. Early in 1942 the Army and Navy announced programs through which qualified students could enlist on an inactive basis and continue their studies until their educational work was completed or until the military needs of the services called them to active duty.

It might be mentioned here that the response of all Columbia students when war came was that of good soldiers. There was no hysteria. Difficult as it was, study continued. On the other hand, there was no attempt to escape service on the ground that one's status as a college student entitled one to a period of deferment. *Spectator,* the College newspaper, speak-

NO WORRIES OVER RATION POINTS
The Midshipmen at Mess

ing for the student body, said in effect: We are ready and await orders to join the armed forces, where we belong. In the meantime, our duty to ourselves, the country, and the University is to get as much out of our lectures and textbooks as we possibly can in the time that remains to us.

Under the Army and Navy plans, with the University Appointments Office acting as military liaison office, students began to enroll in the Army Air Forces Reserve, the Army Enlisted Reserve Corps, the Navy V-1, V-5, and V-7 programs, and the Marine Corps Reserve. Many changed their course of study to include more mathematics and scientific subjects which would better qualify them for officer training. At this time, too, physical education became compulsory for all College students, rather than for freshmen and sophomores only. By the fall of 1942 nearly 1,000 undergraduates had enrolled in one or the other of the reserve programs, while many students from all schools of the University were already on active duty through the draft or enlistment.

Within forty-eight hours of Pearl Harbor, air raid sirens sounded in New York City. Police cars raced through the streets sounding the alarm and thousands of people, instead of taking cover, rushed into the streets. No one really knew whether bombs would ever fall on the city; no one could be sure they wouldn't fall at any moment. So in civilian defense, too, the University was ready. Two months before Pearl Harbor, in keeping with its policy of complete coöperation with the government, the University had set up a Civilian Defense Council. A month before war came, on November 10, 1941, the Council issued its first bulletin, out-

GETTING IN SHAPE FOR ACTION
Naval Calisthenics on South Field

lining its plans and informing the University community of the air raid precautions which were being taken.

The Council's plans went beyond passive defense against air raids. This first bulletin announced three free courses to begin shortly: in first aid; on maintenance of essential services; and on incendiary and demolition bombs. Early in 1942 two of these courses were repeated and a new one, on air raid protection for the home, was offered. At the same time the Council presented a series of five lectures by faculty members and alumni entitled "An American in a World War." Several hundred New York City policemen and air raid wardens attended these courses and 142 neighboring communities were invited to send official representatives. The University, at the urgent request of the Police Department, supplied from its staff and students 119 instructors to assist the police in training wardens. Besides this defense work, the campus had been active for many months in war relief work; the various branches of this service were shortly combined and coördinated in the Columbia University Committee for War Relief. Columbia University Press spread the work of the Civilian Defense Council abroad through publication of a series of pamphlets, the Columbia Home Front Warbooks.

The framework for air raid defense which already existed on December 7, 1941, was enlarged and completed. Thorough organization throughout the University provided for the safety of faculty, students, and property. A Student Auxiliary Corps, to perform first aid, fire-fighting, and messenger work, was organized. In the days when the occurrence of air raids loomed as an imminent possibility, the University's protective organization numbered nearly 1,000 active participants.

The least-known but far from the least important war work carried on by Columbia centers in the, to outsiders, mysterious Division of War Research. The University's facil-

ities in physics, chemistry, engineering, metallurgy, geology, and medical sciences are now largely devoted to this research work. Some of it is performed on the basis of contracts with the national Office of Scientific Research and Development, which was established to conduct experiments on the materials and instrumentalities of war as requested by the armed services. Some of the work is done directly for the War and the Navy Department.

Many faculty members are now wholly engaged in this research. In addition the University has brought together many hundreds of very competent scientists and engineers as members of the Division's staff. They are assisted by another large group of technicians, laboratory workers, and administrative assistants. Large areas of several campus buildings are now given over to the work—and are closely guarded. Numerous contracts are also being carried out at the College of Physicians and Surgeons. Large laboratories are operated at New London, Conn., and at Mineola, Long Island, with smaller stations at a number of other points on both the Atlantic and Pacific Coasts—points which cannot be named until hostilities cease. The range of subject matter of immediate assistance to the prosecution of the war runs through medicine (and its underlying biological sciences), chemistry, physics, mathematics, biophysics, psychology, geology, metallurgy, and engineering (electrical, mechanical, civil, and chemical).

So diverse and so widespread is this scientific work that it has been necessary to take over office space in buildings in several parts of New York City. Each project is in charge of a scientific director, and a committee appointed by President Butler has general supervision of the work. To facilitate the financial administration of the Division of War Research and of other government projects at Columbia, a special Government Contracts Division has been set up in the office of the treasurer of the University.

The Axis would give a good deal to learn just what goes on in the laboratories of the Division of War Research. No one not directly in the work will know until the war is over, but when the story can be told it should be an exciting one and one of which Columbia can be proud.

The Technical Division of the Army's Chemical Warfare Service has expanded its research facilities by the establishment of research centers in widely separated localities in the United States. One of these is at Columbia University. The Laboratories are staffed by qualified officer and civilian personnel, and equipment and other facilities are available for research and test work in chemistry, metallurgy, mechanical and related branches of engineering. Although for reasons of military security no details can be told at this time, the work at the C.W.S. Columbia Laboratories includes investigations on incendiaries, munitions, and related projects, and the personnel act as consultants in manufacturing problems. Lieutenant Colonel Ralph H. Talmage is commanding officer of the Columbia project.

Bard College at Annandale-on-Hudson has taken on the appearance of an Army camp. On August 9, 1943, Bard began the training of 293 enlisted men in the Army Specialized Training Program. These students in uniform constitute the 3223d Service Command Service Unit and are under the command of Major Harvey N. Brown. One group of the trainees is enrolled for basic engineering, and another for the foreign language and area curriculum. The pre-engineering course comprises a heavy schedule of mathematics, physics, and chemistry, and in addition a number of hours are devoted to English, history, and geography. The foreign language curriculum emphasizes mainly the mastery of one spoken language, French or German, and requires intensive drill in the colloquial speech. Two hours a day groups of nine or ten men practice with a native speaker of the language, and five additional hours a week are devoted to study of the grammar and syntax necessary for conversation. The curriculum also requires ten hours of classes a week in the geography, history, and institutions of the areas in which the languages are spoken. In this connection the Bard social science faculty has planned entirely new courses aimed at preparing the men for life among European peoples.

Bard's dormitories are packed as never before. Although there are now only about forty civilian students, the college dining room is, in all, serving about 400 people at each meal instead of the former maximum of 175.

At the School of Nursing, forty students are enrolled in the United States Cadet Nurse Corps, while 165 alumnae are on duty with the armed forces in practically every theater of war. Two of these nurses are prisoners of the Japanese in the Philippines. Two Greek graduates are now aiding their countrymen in Greece. The staff of 120 nurses of General Hospital Number Two, which is now in England, was recruited from the alumnae and graduate staff of the Columbia-Presbyterian Medical Center. On the home front the school's activities have included the teaching of first aid classes, Red Cross Volunteer Nurses' Aides, and home nursing. As part of a wartime accelerated program for college women entering the nursing profession, the school has been affiliated for the past three summers with the Bryn Mawr College Summer School of Nursing.

The Navy Moves In

On April 20, 1942, the Navy "came aboard" Columbia and the most colorful as well as one of the most important of the University's contributions to winning the war began. The

NO DUST ALLOWED
Room Inspection

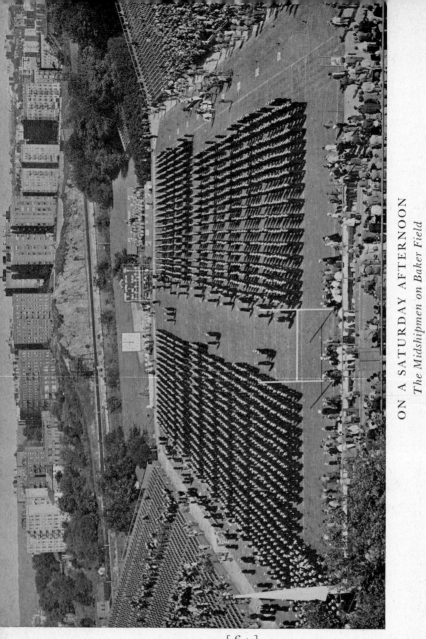

ON A SATURDAY AFTERNOON
The Midshipmen on Baker Field

boarding party was the United States Naval Reserve Midshipmen's School of New York.

What is now the largest school of its kind in the country. turning out 7,500 ensigns a year to man the fighting ships of the fleet, made its first public appearance on June 25, 1940. when President Roosevelt announced to the nation that the Navy was about to inaugurate an emergency, voluntary plan for training 5,000 ensigns a year. By July 16, recruiting for the first group was completed and the first quota of V-7 candidates, as the Navy labeled its program, started on a four-week training cruise. On August 5 the U. S. Naval Reserve Midshipmen's School at New York was officially established and on August 10 the first class of 298 apprentice seamen came aboard the arklike *Prairie State.*

At this time the school had no connection with Columbia, but the *Prairie State,* tied up at 135th Street in the Hudson, was a near and familiar neighbor. The ship is the former U. S. battleship *Illinois,* launched in 1898 and once the pride of the Navy in the days of the Great White Fleet.

The school's first class was commissioned on November 14, 1940, and the second class entered only eight days later. The fifth class was more than halfway through its training period when the Japanese struck at Pearl Harbor, and in its sixteen months of existence the school had turned out over 1,500 officers. Although classes had grown larger, the *Prairie State* was still the only home of the school's activities. The Navy had, however, long foreseen the expansion necessary if the country actually got into the "shooting war." Even as the school was being opened in the summer of 1940, the Navy was looking for facilities into which to expand if such a step should become necessary; at the same time the University's new Committee on National Defense, as one of its first acts, offered its coöperation to the Navy. The final result was that on February 21, 1941, more than a year before the Navy actually moved onto the Columbia campus, and unknown to the general public, the Navy and the University signed an agreement providing for the use of Columbia buildings and facilities "if and when it is declared necessary by the Secretary of the Navy as a war measure." The University needed no urging to "agree to consider this training of primary importance during the continuance of the national emergency making it necessary."

In December, 1941, the Navy decided that by the next summer it would be ready to move into Johnson Hall and to train 600 men there. Actually, by August, 1942, one class had already graduated from the Columbia school and 2,000 more midshipmen and apprentice seamen were on the campus. It had become clear that the expanding Navy's need for officers was exceeding even the great plans previously made, and the utmost in action and coöperation was called for from the school and Columbia to speed up the program. Thus it was that the first Columbia class of 300 men—the school's seventh class—made Furnald Hall, rather than Johnson, its ship-on-land training quarters.

But even this was not enough. On July 2, as the result of further special effort on the part of the University and the Navy, 900 apprentice seamen moved into John Jay Hall which had been made ready on less than a month's notice. In the end, Johnson Hall, which the Navy took over in August, 1942, was the last, not the first, of Columbia's dormitories to be occupied; and as the first men moved in, the first Columbia class moved out of Furnald, ensign commissions in hand. In the meantime, the planned capacity of Johnson and of Furnald had been considerably increased by the installation of double decker bunks.

More than dormitory facilities were required by the Navy and supplied by Columbia: the midshipmen mess in the John Jay Hall Dining Room and in Johnson Hall; they use East Hall, Journalism, Hamilton, and half a dozen other buildings for classes; they share the gymnasium and swim-

THE NAVY WATCHES WITH INTEREST
In the Baker Field Stands

ming pool, and Earl Hall, the recreation center, with Columbia students. The earth of South Field has been packed concrete-hard by thousands of midshipmen using it for drill, athletics, and review.

From that first 1940 class of 298 men, the school has grown to a midshipmen regiment of 2,600, with 350 officers (about eighty of them receiving instruction), and 450 enlisted personnel, including WAVES. Each class now commissioned numbers from 1,000 to 1,200 ensigns; the school's fifteenth class graduated in November, 1943. To that date almost 12,000 ensigns had gone from the school to the fleet, a tremendous number when it is remembered that not much more than three years ago the entire line officer complement of the U. S. Navy on active duty was 7,650 men. Today one out of every fifteen officers in the Navy is a graduate of the

[67]

Columbia school. Most of these new ensigns go to sea without ever having been aboard a real ship of the Navy, but with the entry of the eleventh class the school for the first time had as officer candidates a considerable number of enlisted men—185—who had already been on active duty.

The day of a V-7 trainee begins long before the University's normal operations come to life—at 5:30 A. M., in fact—and ends at 10 P. M. The men march to classes, march to mess, march to the drill field—they march all week and end up on Saturday morning with a review and inspection on South Field that is an eagerly awaited occasion and always draws a crowd to hear the school band and to admire the precise movements of the battalions.

The future officers enter as apprentice seamen and during the first three weeks marching drills, practice in pulling whaleboats, and gun drills are present in large quantities. All students take a special mathematics course, while another course acquaints them with Navy nomenclature, customs, and traditions. As apprentice seamen, the men are under very close scrutiny, and only those who show definite officer qualities are continued in training.

After three weeks the men are sworn in as midshipmen and start the stiffest three months of their lives. Ninety percent study to be deck officers, the rest engineering officers. They study navigation, seamanship, communications, ordnance, and damage control—four hours of classes, six of study every day. In addition they participate in frequent physical drills, first aid classes, and boat and gun drills. Technical films are used with great success, and while the midshipmen do not learn everything they would at Annapolis, what they do learn is modern and eminently practical. They gain some shipboard experience on day-long cruises aboard the Navy's

COLUMBIA COLLEGE SCENE, PRE-WAR
Students on Hamilton Hall Steps

[69]

fast little YP patrol boats. Here they stand watches, take sights, run through general quarters, fire, and lifeboat drills. And some of them get very, very seasick. Trips to the Navy Yard and lectures by such practical specialists as Lieutenant Commander Bulkeley on PT boats bring them in close touch with the active duty that awaits them.

The midshipmen still manage, in spite of such a schedule as this, to find some time for social life—dances, visits to radio broadcasts, "shore leave" from the USS Furnald, John Jay, Johnson, and *Prairie State*. Each class even publishes its own "yearbook," the *Side Boy*.

Upon graduation most of the new ensigns go to sea at once, although some are sent to other naval stations for further specialized training. They are inexperienced, and admittedly their training has been of an emergency nature. But they can—and have—fought in the best traditions of the American Navy. Already they have won citations—and suffered casualties. By November, 1943, the records show, there had been 135 casualties among graduates of the Midshipmen's School. Ten of these are known to have been killed in action; forty-seven have been officially declared dead after being reported missing in action; and five others are presumed to have been killed although their fate has not been finally and officially determined. Forty-seven more are missing in action; fifteen have been wounded in action and two in accidents; and nine are prisoners of war.

Eighteen graduates have earned honors and decorations such as the Navy Cross, the Silver Star, and the Navy and Marine Medal, while to one has gone, posthumously, the rarely awarded highest honor of all, the Congressional Medal of Honor. He was Ensign Herbert C. Jones, of the first class to be commissioned from the school, and the cita-

tion tells the story of his "conspicuous devotion to duty, extraordinary courage, and complete disregard to his own life, above and beyond the call of duty," during the Japanese attack on Pearl Harbor on December 7, 1941:

"Ensign Jones organized and led a party, which was supplying ammunition to the anti-aircraft battery of the USS *California* after the mechanical hoists were put out of action, when he was fatally wounded by a bomb explosion. When two men attempted to take him from the area which was on fire he refused to let them do so, saying in words to the effect, 'Leave me alone! I am done for. Get out of here before the magazines go off.'"

The first commanding officer of the school was Captain John J. London, U.S.N. (Ret.). He was succeeded in January, 1942, shortly before the school enveloped Columbia, by

STUDYING FOR UNCLE SAM
V-12 Seamen in Class

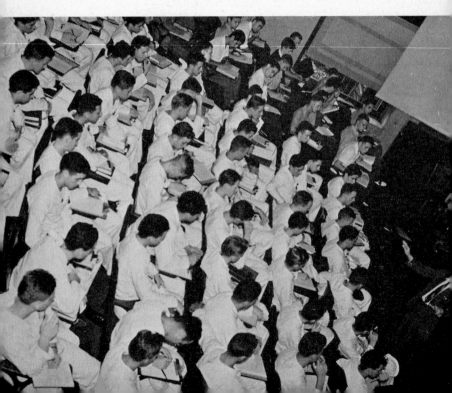

Commander, now Captain, John K. Richards, U.S.N. (Ret.), who today is one of the most familiar figures on the campus. Captain Richards, who graduated from the Naval Academy in 1912, has seen duty on all kinds of ships and in all parts of the world. When the *Jacob Jones* was torpedoed in the English Channel in the cold of December, 1917, it was Lieutenant Richards who "did much to keep up the men's spirits," the men being those lucky few of the crew who survived the explosion and the following seventeen hours in the water. At the close of the war he was commanding his own destroyer, and at the time of his retirement in 1933 he was flag secretary to Vice Admiral William H. Standley.

Early in July, 1943, another unit came aboard Columbia. This group of young men in Navy blue and white represented the V-12 Navy College program, designed to give specialized training, from the ground up where necessary, in medicine, engineering, and other subjects. It is the Navy's counterpart of the Army Specialized Training Program. Five hundred and forty-six men entered with this first Columbia V-12 group, of whom 316 were registered in Columbia College and 230 in the School of Engineering. About 120 of those in the College were on the campus of an institution of higher learning for the first time in their lives. The others had previously been civilian students, about one-third of them at Columbia, while about a dozen came to school from active duty with the fleet. Of the whole number, 117 are following the pre-medical course. The others are either engineering or pre-engineering students.

This V-12 trainee is an entirely new kind of college student. He is in uniform, an apprentice seaman in the Naval Reserve, and differs from other enlisted men in the Navy only in the duties assigned to him and in the use which the Navy hopes eventually to make of him. He receives Navy pay and housing, messing, uniforms, and equipment, including textbooks. Like any sailor, he is subject to all Navy regulations and orders, and he lives under regular Navy discipline.

The apprentice seamen are housed in Hartley and Livingston Halls, thus completing the occupation of all the men's dormitories. They mess in the pre-war Lion's Den in John Jay. They are kept on their toes by daily naval activity and discipline, but it is continually borne in mind that their primary duty is to study for future service with the fleet. Reveille is at six o'clock; they form on South Field for twenty minutes of calisthenics; then shave and dress and form in sections for morning mess. After mess they prepare their rooms for inspection (Columbia's dormitory rooms were never in history so neat and ship-shape as they are these days) and then proceed to classes. At the noon hour comes inspection as well as mess. The afternoons are devoted largely to shop and laboratory work, and the evenings to study. Lights go out at 10:30.

While the Navy's chief purpose must be to prepare these men for their special duties with the fleet at the earliest possible moment, technical and professional subjects are not their only studies. In devising the V-12 Program the Navy kept constantly in mind that useful citizens and officers have to be more than skilled technicians. So far as the exigencies of war will allow, the course of study was planned accordingly. All first-term pre-engineering students take English and history, as well as mathematics, physics, drafting, and physical education. In the first term of the pre-medical course, English and history are postponed in favor of chemistry and French or German. Those men who started at some point beyond the first term of college work take the regular courses offered by the College and the School of Engineering. The work in English is chiefly composition and oral practice, while the course in history is an interesting presentation of the historical background of the war, planned and taught by the Contemporary Civilization staff of the College.

All personnel service of the College is fully available to

AN ADMIRAL LOOKS THEM OVER
The V-12 Unit in Review

the V-12 boys, and at the time of entrance each one is assigned to a faculty adviser who attempts to serve as counselor
and friend in exactly the same way as for civilian students.
Such special services as instruction in reading techniques
are at the Navy men's disposal. Personal and scholastic records of every man are kept in the dean's office, exactly as is
the practice for regular students.

Most of the first group of students are residents of the
metropolitan area, since it is the Navy's policy to assign a
man within the Naval District in which he lives. In addition,
each trainee is invited to express a college preference. The
spirit of the unit is good, in spite of the unusually heavy
physical and mental burden which seemed staggering to
some at first. Many of the seamen have entered into the extracurricular and social life of the College, which is what both

the College and the Navy hoped for. Many members of the 1943 football squad were V-12 men.

Following naval practice, Captain Richards, as senior officer present, is the commanding officer of the V-12 unit as well as of the Midshipmen's School. The actual administration of the unit is in the hands of Commander Dallas Grover as officer-in-charge.

As has been the case in all of Columbia's dealings with the Navy, the relationships brought about by the V-12 Program have been happy ones. After the first unit had been on campus for some time, Associate Dean Nicholas M. McKnight of the College said: "The V-12 Program is soundly conceived and, with careful administration, both naval and academic, can attain the objects for which the Navy established it. From the University's viewpoint, we can properly feel that through participation in the program we are making direct

SAILORS' APPETITES ARE GOOD
The V-12 Boys at Mess

and useful contribution to the war program and are at the same time continuing to perform our normal functions in the area of undergraduate instruction." Incidentally, Columbia College and the other schools of the University still have civilian students—students not yet eighteen or students deferred for physical disability or other reasons.

Up at the Medical Center, the College of Physicians and Surgeons and the School of Dental and Oral Surgery also have students in uniform—both Army and Navy. Nearly 600 enlisted men are now studying in the two schools: 287 Army men and 114 Navy men in P. & S.; 142 and 39 respectively in the Dental School. The sailors are part of the V-12 Program, while the soldiers are the 3209th Service Command Service Unit of the Army Specialized Training Program. The soldiers are under the command of Lieutenant Colonel Mark R. M. Gwilliam.

The story of the Navy at Columbia is not complete without mention of three other less well known but important activities. First in point of time is the School of Officers' Indoctrination, which was instituted in May, 1942, to prepare specialist officers for duty as instructors in the Midshipmen's School. To this end 244 commissioned officers were put through a comprehensive course covering much the same ground as the midshipman curriculum. The next job of the School of Indoctrination was to give a six-week course to 265 officers who have now been sent to all parts of the United States as administrators for the V-12 program. Actually, this unit was trained off campus in the Supply Annex near the *Prairie State,* but neither the Navy nor Columbia bothers any longer to try to distinguish between Columbia and non-Columbia naval projects on Morningside Heights. It is all one job, with just one purpose.

The second of these special Navy units is the School of Military Government and Administration, which is administered from one of the University's small buildings on 117th

Street, across the street from Johnson Hall, now the headquarters of all Navy activity at Columbia. Shortly after the
outbreak of war, the Navy set in motion plans for training
officers to administer and govern conquered and reconquered
areas in the Pacific. Columbia was chosen as the location for
this training, and the first twenty-nine officers arrived on
August 17, 1942. Prior to that date a good deal of fast and
furious work had been going on at the University to plan
the curriculum and to provide the necessary instructors. The
burden of this work rested on the shoulders of Professors
Schuyler C. Wallace and Philip C. Jessup, the former becoming director of the school.

Two-thirds of that first group of student-officers had had
experience of one kind or another in the Far East; four of
them were lawyers; two, anthropologists; one a Congressman;
one a political scientist. The curriculum stresses (1) languages; (2) the study of native institutions; (3) an understanding of the colonial institutions to which the native popula-
tions of the Far East have been accustomed; and, (4) certain
technical aspects of military government itself. Drawing upon
the entire language resources of the University, the curriculum provides refresher courses in French, Spanish, Portu-
guese, Dutch, German, Russian, Chinese, and Japanese. Primary attention, though, is directed to the fascinating and
bewildering colloquial Malay and Melanesian Pidgin English so that upon landing on any island of the Southwest
Pacific an officer trained at the School would be able to com-
municate with the natives. Other subjects include geography, anthropology, colonial government, and international
relations. Experts were at hand right at the University in almost every field of interest to the school, but with the desire
of assembling the most effective staff possible other institutions as well as the entire resources of Columbia were drawn
upon. Today, although most of the teaching staff is a part
of the Columbia faculty, almost one-third comes from other

**WHERE THE LOUNGE IS NOW
THE QUARTERDECK**
Johnson Hall, Navy Headquarters

places, some as far distant as California and Hawaii. Instruction has regularly been supplemented by evening lectures given by outsiders with wide experience in special fields.

In less than a year after its start, two other groups of officers joined the "student body," bringing the total to about 100 officers, representing the Marines, the Coast Guard, and the U. S. Public Health Service, as well as the Navy.

The School of Military Government and Administration, so far as the University is officially concerned, is part of the Program of Training in International Administration. Besides the naval branch already described, this program trains civilians for work in European areas and in China. The

THE COMMANDING OFFICER
Captain John K. Richards

[80]

course is designed primarily to aid in the development of personnel equipped to perform tasks of an administrative nature in countries and territories liberated or occupied by the United Nations. While the immediate emphasis is thus upon the emergency tasks resulting from the war, the program is also planned to afford training for persons preparing for post-war careers abroad as representatives of American business firms, in government service, or on the staffs of international organizations. The program as offered in 1942–43 required forty-eight weeks for completion. Now it has been found possible to condense it into two semesters, following the pattern of a normal academic year. Each student chooses a region or area of specialization. For the school year 1943–44 study is being concentrated on France and Belgium, Germany, the Danubian basin and Greece, and China. "This plan," the University's announcement significantly notes, "is subject to change as demand may arise for study in other areas or as changing conditions may dictate." The program is open to both men and women, between twenty-five and fifty-five years of age. Such education as is represented by a degree from an acceptable college or university, or its equivalent, is required for admission. Seventy-three students were accepted for the course in the fall of 1943.

Finally, to complete the account of the Navy at Columbia, mention should be made of the Civilian Orientation Course. The purpose of this course was to introduce the problems, customs, organization, and equipment of the Navy to leaders of those American industries which are entrusted with the production of that equipment. The first session of the course brought together in Earl Hall on February 1, 1943, two dozen representatives of some of America's greatest industries. For three weeks these guests of the Navy attended lectures and movies on every possible subject, from the organization of the Navy Department to bomb disposal. In addition, they were taken to the Navy Yard, to Floyd Bennett Field, to

Quantico, and to New London, Conn., where they went down in a submarine. They were addressed by no less than ten admirals and a number of other distinguished Navy men and professors. A second class of industrialists, twice as large as the first, convened in May.

This story of the Navy's activities at Columbia makes it obvious why Captain Richards is about as busy a person as the campus has ever seen. He is commanding officer of all of these Navy schools, courses, and programs, and has under him the more than 4,000 persons now attached in one way or another to the Naval Reserve Midshipmen's School, including V-12 units at other institutions in New York City. Addressing a gathering of Columbia faculty members recently, Captain Richards summed up the relationship between the Navy and the University in these words:

"So we are here—we the military—to pour into this great well of learning our thoughts of action and purpose, that they may mingle with yours; that together the youth will be strengthened to face reality, to face the world as it is, not as we might wish it to be; for only the future will lift that veil. We will develop the iron hand while you, my colleagues, will groom it with the velvet glove, that civilization will go forward in spite of wars and devastation."

Men and Women of Columbia

Besides the more conspicuous services rendered by Columbia and described above, the University and its individual faculty members are contributing to the winning of the war and the peace in many ways. As a somewhat unusual, but by no means unique, example, might be cited the story behind the Chinese Graduate School of Journalism, sponsored by the Chinese government, which opened in Chungking in October, 1943. The school, designed to fill China's growing need for trained journalists, was the idea of Hollington K. Tong, vice minister of information in Chiang Kai-shek's government and a member of the Columbia School of Journalism class of 1913. He enlisted the aid of his classmate, Dean Carl W. Ackerman, who sent not only textbooks and stationery but also Professor Harold L. Cross, who now heads a faculty of seven Americans (three of them Columbia alumni) and one Chinese.

Any account of Columbia in World War II—so far as history has yet revealed it—would certainly not be complete unless it told of the part played by her alumni and alumnae, including many students who left to enter the armed forces before completing their studies. By February, 1944, 5,500 alumni were known to be in service, and the actual number was probably considerably greater, since it is almost impossible to keep the records completely up-to-date. Of this number more than 3,200 are officers in the Army, Navy, Marine Corps, and Coast Guard, including seven admirals and twelve generals. The best known of these latter is the Air Force's Lieutenant General Ira C. Eaker of the Law School class of 1926. Thirty-four alumni are known to have been killed in action; eleven are missing; and ten are prisoners of war.

HE KEEPS ON ROARING
The Columbia Lion

[83]

III. AFTER "THE DURATION:"
A POSTSCRIPT

What Is Columbia?

"Nothing in the entire course of the history of civilization," wrote the late Herbert E. Hawkes in what was to be his last annual report as dean of Columbia College, "has been as important for humanity as the outcome of the present struggle."

That every part of Columbia University subscribes to this statement is being demonstrated every day by word and by deed. These manifold war activities of the University have already been described, but it is perfectly true that Columbia is not "100 percent engaged in war work," as many industries advertise. It would be unthinkable for an automobile manufacturer in time of war to insist on manufacturing pleasure cars instead of tanks; at the same time, it is his duty to preserve his knowledge of pleasure cars and to be prepared to manufacture them again when peace comes. In the same way, it is a university's duty to devote as much as necessary and as much as possible of its physical and mental resources to winning the war; yet the university has just as great a duty to keep alive its normal functions and to look ahead to the future.

For waging war is not the true function of a university, important as its aid can be in modern warfare. In fact, were war a permanent condition of life, universities would, in time, cease to exist. No institutions and no individuals need and desire peace more than universities and scholars. Today the university and the scholar help fight, not for the sake of fighting, not just for the sake of winning the war, but primarily with the hope of establishing the kind of peace without which existence would be meaningless for a real university or a true scholar. Columbia, therefore, believes that not only must this war be won, but that out of it must come a peace that will enable it to get out of uniform—and stay out—so that it can again fulfill its real purpose in life. This does not by any means imply that Columbia University is thinking in terms of "back to normalcy." No one is better aware than those entrusted with the management of a university that the only permanent thing in life is change. A university, dedicated to the preservation, dissemination, and, above all, the advancement of knowledge, knows that it is not today what it was yesterday, that it will not be tomorrow what it is today. A university that remains static dies; it is not then a university, for it is supposed to be an active agent helping to bring about change—for the better—in man's ways of life, physical, mental, and moral. A university is not interested in passively accepting change; its duty as well as its interest is in helping shape the change in things to come. Today, American universities are just as actively engaged in searching self-inquiry and in planning for the future as they are in the war. They know this war is going to make a profound alteration in the ways of the world, and so they know their job is bigger than ever. Columbia is very definitely engaged in facing this problem, but to know what Columbia will be and hopes to be after the war, it is necessary to understand what Columbia is and has been. The best starting point is the name itself: *Columbia University in the City of New York.*

Columbia: The word is a symbol of America, but behind it are the history and traditions of the English-speaking world and the whole heritage of western civilization. In its

THE HEART OF THE CAMPUS
Low Memorial Library

[86]

use here it evokes the memories of an institution's long and honorable existence, of its evolution and development through the years.

University: The most significant part of this evolution and development has been the growth of Columbia from a college to a university. A university is not necessarily a better institution than any other kind of educational organism, but, if it is a true university, it is at least different. A university is not just an undergraduate college, it is not just a technical and vocational school, it is not just a professional school, it is not just a graduate school. A university—an American university, that is, for we are not here concerned with European institutions of higher learning which have evolved along a different path—is all of these things, and, in a sense, something more, something rather intangible. The over-all size of a university is not the important thing; nor the size of a particular part. It is the completeness, the unity, and the integration of the whole institution which determine its right to the honorable title of university. Such an organization defies the laws of nature, for the whole *is* greater than the sum of its parts.

A complete university does not stress the arts and neglect the sciences; it does not lavish attention on one school at the expense of another. It does provide the organization, the facilities, and the instructors necessary to teaching and research from the college freshman year to the most advanced graduate study. Columbia University, as an examination of its organizational structure or the catalogues of its various schools and departments shows, is, by this test, a complete university.

An institution may, however, have all the parts specified above and still not deserve high rank as a university. Unity and integration of the parts are as important as the parts themselves. And if a high degree of unity and integration is achieved, the usefulness and efficiency of each part will be

[87]

multiplied many times. Columbia has had growing pains in the course of its life. The task of achieving unity and integration while expanding in all directions has been a delicate one, but it has been accomplished.

It is impossible here to describe completely the theory and the practice by which Columbia University in its day-to-day operations functions as a true university. Something has already been said above about the top organizational arrangement of trustees and University Council. Various publications of the University and the annual catalogues tell how unity and integration come about in the relations of different schools and departments to each other and to the University. A few examples may be cited here to show what is done, and why.

Each member of the faculty is officially assigned to a particular school or department, but his wisdom and experience are available to any other school. A member of the Graduate Faculties staff may teach a course or help in a seminar in the College. Thus each part shares in talent which alone it could not afford.

The transition from undergraduate to graduate or professional study is planned in advance. When a student goes from one of the University's undergraduate schools to a professional or graduate school, he does not find himself in a new and strange world. He does not find that he took the wrong courses in his sophomore year. What he has already accomplished is not something useless which must be discarded but rather is a solid foundation for the next step up the educational ladder. This is achieved in various ways. For example, Columbia College does not educate those who want to be engineers without regard to the requirements of the School of Engineering. The proper background of science and mathematics is provided. On the other hand, the School of Engineering cannot, and would not if it could, compel the College to teach its pre-engineering students only

FROM LOW TO JOHN JAY
A View Across the Campus

science and mathematics. Engineering wants the College to
send it men who have a sound background in the humanities
and the social sciences as well as in the physical sciences. In
the same way, the College sends to the Law School students
who have the foundation in history, government, and soci-
ology necessary to the proper study of law in modern society.
Another good example of integration is the system whereby
students in the College can arrange their work so that the
fourth year in the College is also the first in a professional
school.

At the same time, it should be noted that neither Columbia College nor Barnard College is in business merely as a
feeder for the professional and graduate schools. They offer
to those who want it, and who may have no intention of going further, the best type of modern liberal arts education.

The Columbia College curriculum, by way of illustration,
is based on the assumption that each student is both a mem-

MODERN HOME OF THE HEALING ARTS
The Columbia-Presbyterian Medical Center

ber of society in which he must learn to take his place and play his part and an individual with his own personal needs, desires, and abilities. The first two years of the College curriculum—the Lower College—treat him primarily as a member of society: he takes broad courses in the social sciences, the physical sciences, and the humanities; he demonstrates his proficiency in English and in some foreign language. The second two years—the Upper College—concentrate on him as an individual: on the broad but solid foundation of the first two years he can specialize to the extent of his abilities and in whatever direction his future scholarly or professional interests are to take him.

As Harry J. Carman, dean of the College, expresses it, the undergraduate study of the liberal arts should be "part of the basic principles of the mental equipment of every educated person. A consequence of graduating men and women who had majored in one subject to the exclusion of all others would be turning out students who were technically trained, sometimes to work efficiently in a very narrow field, but with little interest in the cultural implications of their profession, and much less in those things which would enable them to formulate for themselves a satisfying philosophy of life."

Nor are the professional schools interested merely in turning out good technicians. The School of Engineering wants to graduate the most competent engineers possible; the College of Physicians and Surgeons, the most competent doctors; but these schools also want engineers and doctors who understand the relation of their professions to the political, economic, and social life of the nation and the world. The School of Journalism believes that a Washington correspondent cannot today write intelligently about our Federal Government's daily activities unless he knows the history and philosophy which lie behind our political system. Accordingly, its requirements and its curriculum are arranged to

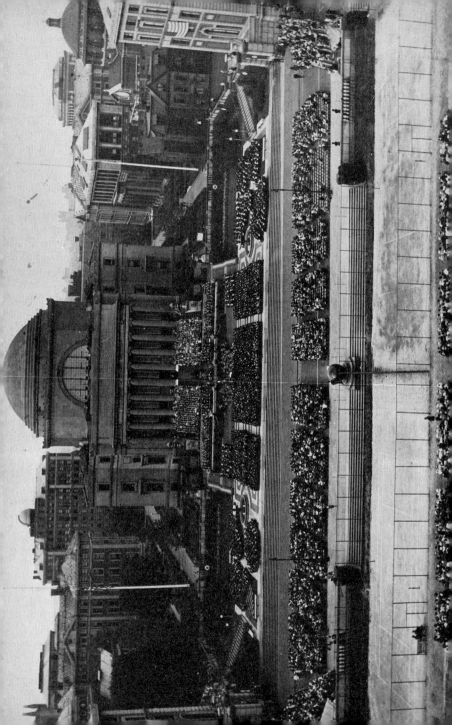

provide this background. The Law School is not interested in competent law-book technicians. It bases its curriculum on the teaching of law in its relation to man as a social, political, and economic being. The same principles are followed throughout the other professional and graduate schools to the end that human beings will finish their educational careers with some degree of understanding of other human beings and the world we humans live in, as well as with technical and professional competence in their chosen fields. This is the only worthwhile end which the completeness, the unity, and the integration of any university can hope to achieve.

In the City of New York: When the trustees of Columbia University changed the corporate name to recognize the university status which had been reached, they very deliberately included this phrase. For this is an important part of the institution's name, not a geographical label. It is a symbol of the third factor in the history of the institution's growth and development. Some mention of this has already been made. Here it is only necessary to emphasize that Columbia University does not try to ignore the City of New York. It could not if it would; and it would not if it could. The city is a stimulating influence on the University; the University is by no means without influence in the life of the city. The city is a throbbing center of activity in all aspects of life, and the University deliberately and to good purpose makes use of this fact. The city is an immense laboratory for faculty and students. Furthermore, Columbia students, when they become alumni, will have to live in and with the world exemplified by the city. They start that process of adjustment while they are students.

These paragraphs, although very far from telling the whole

DEGREES ARE AWARDED OUTDOORS
The Commencement Day Scene

THE NAVY HAS MOVED IN HERE
Hartley, Livingston, John Jay

story, will, it is hoped, help explain the meaning of *Columbia University in the City of New York.*

What Will Columbia Be?

But what of the Columbia University of the future? No one knows what the next few years will bring. A university does not pretend to have special and supernatural sources of information. But its collective experience and competence enable it to exercise judgment and to proceed with reasonable hope in its efforts to mold the pattern of its future. This implies the fundamental assumption on the part of the University that it is not satisfied to sit by and wait *to be* changed. That is true. The University knows a different world is in the making, and it wants to have something to say about that world and about its place in it. To that end, officers and teachers, as individuals and in groups, are already planning the post-war Columbia. Not that it will be fundamentally a different institution, for there is no reason it should. But there will be changed conditions, both within and without the University, new factors, new needs, new problems. There will even be valuable experience gained through participation in the war.

ON THE CAMPUS, WINTER
The Van Amringe Quadrangle

In Columbia College a committee of faculty members is already at work studying the present curriculum in the light of what changes should and must be made after the war. Particular attention is being paid to the needs of returning service men. A similar faculty group in the Law School is studying the future of legal education. The School of Engineering is mapping its post-war policy "as an entirely new problem—as if we were setting up a new engineering school." The School of Business has already formulated a post-war program to permit returning service men to resume their studies under a special curriculum. So it goes throughout the University. This process of thinking and planning ahead is reflected in the thinking and writing of every Columbia dean. Here, as samples, not as exceptional cases, is what a few have had to say recently concerning these important problems:

"Building activity in the near future," predicts Dean Leopold Arnaud of the School of Architecture, "will be tremendous in scope; and because the changes in methods and forms will be drastic and general, it should be a period of great creative fecundity. New methods, new materials, new problems, new social and economic requirements will produce not only a new era, but also a new physical world."

James Kip Finch, associate dean of the School of Engineering, notes that: "Shortages of all kinds, from homes to refrigerators and from motor cars to clothing, plus a wide distribution of purchasing power, should make possible a real period of post-war prosperity. . . . Our engineering schools must, therefore, turn their attention to training their students for the requirements of this new and promising era. The older, still largely empirical, standardized handbook practices and methods of the past will not carry the engineer very far in an age of new materials and methods which will require new techniques, and active and constructive imaginative powers. Both a trained imagination, backed up by a

[96]

ON THE CAMPUS, SPRING
The Van Amringe Quadrangle
[97]

thorough knowledge of basic principles and skill in using the latest tools of technical analysis, as well as sound judgment, and ability to keep one's feet on the ground, will be required in these days to come."

"Victory for the United Nations," asserts Dean Robert D. Calkins of the School of Business, "will create a new era of American leadership and participation in world affairs. . . . A new type of international businessman will be needed. . . . Schools of business must retreat from their paramount interest in education for business as we have known it, and emphasize their more fundamental objective which is to educate men and women to operate the economic system of tomorrow through whatever business or other operating units it is to function."

Finally, let President Nicholas Murray Butler sum up the role of the University in the post-war world which it will be called upon to help establish and stabilize:

"In the new organization of the world for the protection of prosperity and peace against any other attack similar to that which is now going forward on so stupendous a scale, the colleges and universities must be everywhere a guiding influence. . . . A reconstructed world will rest upon a sound basis of economic, social and political principles, and be supported by intellectual convictions and confidence. Here again is the impressive task which confronts the American colleges and universities during the years immediately to come."

In these statements it is significant that there is no defeatism. Although there is no shrinking from the problems that will have to be faced, they are being faced with practical optimism. The coming of victory will find Columbia University ready to do its share and to adjust itself to a changed world. In the midst of the most terrible conflict of all time, but with a confident eye on the future, Columbia University, her officers, teachers, students, and alumni find more com-

fort and more meaning than ever in the words of their Alma
Mater song, *Stand Columbia:*

> Mother, stayed on rock eternal,
> Crowned and set upon a height
> Glorified by light supernal—
> In thy radiance we see light.
> Torch, thy children's lamps to kindle,
> Beacon-star, to cheer and guide,
> Stand, Columbia! Alma Mater—
> Through the storms of Time abide!
>
> Mighty patriots, warriors, sages,
> Thou hast borne, a shining band;
> Teach thy sons in future ages
> Still to love their native land.
> Throned upon the hill where heroes
> Fought for Liberty, and died,
> Stand, Columbia! Alma Mater—
> Through the storms of Time abide!

SYMBOL OF THE UNIVERSITY
The Alma Mater Statue

[99]

For certain of the illustrations in this book credit is due: Fairchild Aerial Surveys, Geo. P. Hall & Son, Wide World Photos, John Mladinov, Jack M. Lewis, J. Boldtman, Delar, Underwood and Underwood, U. S. Navy, Maurice Emerson, Gábor Éder, William Frange, and A. Tennyson Beals. The portrait of President Butler is by Sir William Orpen.